A BEAUTIFUL BOUQUET

Rebellion, Reflection, and Renewal

Sheresse Winford

Struggles to Success
A Series of Hope and Inspiration

A Series of Hope and Inspiration

® Copyright 2024. Sheresse Winford.

All rights reserved. No portion of this book may be reproduced by mechanical, photographic, or electronic process, nor may it be stored in a retrieval system, transmitted in any form or otherwise be copied for public or private use without written permission of the copyright owner.

For more information contact:
www.figfactormedia.com

Cover Design and Layout by DG Marco Antonio Álvarez Rodríguez
Printed in the United States of America

ISBN: 978-1-961600-38-6

Library of Congress Control Number: 2024921294

A BEAUTIFUL BOUQUET

Rebellion, Reflection, and Renewal

Dedication

To my children, Roynetta Tripp, Tevin Winford (forever in my heart), Davion Winford, Ryan Winford, and Ciera Winford.

You are the roots of our family, the flowers in my bouquet, the strength that grounds me, and the love that blooms in every chapter of my life.

This book is for you with love, a testament to the resilience and beauty we've built together.

Table of Contents

6	Acknowledgments
8	Introduction
11	Chapter 1: The Growing Pains of Youth
15	Chapter 2: The Joy of School Days
19	Chapter 3: Discovering Freedom Through Friendship
23	Chapter 4: Lessons in Self-Discovery
27	Chapter 5: Running Toward Independence
31	Chapter 6: Finding Strength in Unexpected Places
35	Chapter 7: The Redemption of Second Chances
39	Chapter 8: Embracing Change and Growth
43	Chapter 9: Rewriting My Story
47	Chapter 10: Building Bridges, Not Walls
51	Chapter 11: Rediscovering My Strength
55	Chapter 12: My Journey to Redemption
58	About the Author

Acknowledgments

To Joann Barnes and my newfound friends from *Building on a Design for Living*—thank you for your support and encouragement on this journey.

To my Pastor, John Hannah, thank you for teaching me the power of perseverance and the importance of finishing what you start. Your guidance has been a light unto my path, and I am forever grateful for your wisdom and inspiration.

Introduction

A *Beautiful Bouquet: Rebellion, Reflection, and Redemption* is a continuation of Sheresse Winford's transformative life journey—a reflection on the rebellious phases of adolescence and how they shaped her path toward self-awareness and empowerment. This book takes you through the complicated terrain of youth, where mistakes, defiance, and missteps are not just part of the process but essential for growth. Sheresse's story is a powerful reminder that rebellion, while often seen as negative, can be a necessary part of finding one's true self.

In this second installment, Sheresse takes readers back to her teenage years, a time filled with confusion, rebellion, and the search for independence. Her decisions—whether to defy her mother's wishes, run away from home, or hang out with the wrong crowd—were all steps in her journey of self-discovery. This book emphasizes that mistakes are not failures but opportunities to learn. Each rebellious act allowed Sheresse to understand more about herself, her values, and what she truly wanted from life.

A *Beautiful Bouquet* reframes the concept of rebellion. Instead of focusing on regret, Sheresse invites readers to see rebellion as an expression of independence and exploration. For her, these moments of defiance were the seeds of empowerment and the beginning of her journey toward self-awareness. Adolescence was a time of searching, and even when her choices led her down difficult paths, they ultimately guided her toward clarity and redemption.

This book isn't just about looking back. It's about how those early experiences shaped the woman Sheresse is today. Her friendships, the joy of school, and even her mistakes were all critical elements of her personal growth. While some relationships and decisions led her astray, they taught her invaluable lessons about independence, loyalty, and responsibility. She learned that finding freedom sometimes meant breaking the rules, but ultimately led her to a deeper understanding of what true freedom means—self-reliance and accountability.

The heart of *A Beautiful Bouquet* lies in its message of redemption. Sheresse's journey shows that no matter how far we stray, there is always a way back. The mistakes we make in life don't have to define us; instead, they can become stepping stones toward a better future. Sheresse's return home, her decision to go back to school, and her eventual work toward a GED all reflect her determination to rewrite her story.

Each chapter of this book is paired with a reflective question, allowing you to engage with Sheresse's experiences on a personal level. These questions prompt introspection, encouraging you to see your own moments of rebellion not as something to regret but as vital pieces of your personal growth. Reflecting on your mistakes and challenges will inspire you to embrace your journey with the same courage and determination that Sheresse did.

In *A Beautiful Bouquet*, you will find:

- A fresh perspective on rebellion as a powerful tool for self-discovery and growth.
- The importance of friendships and how they influence the choices we make.
- It is a story of redemption, proving zthat second chances are possible for everyone.
- An invitation to reflect on your life choices and the lessons you have learned from them.

Sheresse's story in *A Beautiful Bouquet* is a testament to the power of reflection and self-forgiveness. She shows us that even when life seems messy and out of control, we can course-correct and find a path toward redemption. This book offers us both hope and practical wisdom on how to turn our mistakes into a beautiful bouquet—a life that is richer, fuller, and filled with purpose.

Chapter 1:

The Growing Pains of Youth

Adolescence is a season of change—a time when we're trying to figure out who we are in a world that often feels confusing and challenging, and that was only made worse when my dad died in a swimming accident just before my 8th-grade graduation. On top of that pain, or perhaps in response to it, my teenage years were marked by a rebellious spirit, but that defiance was more than just a phase. It was my way of seeking independence, a way of exploring who I was and what I believed in. I didn't realize it then, but each rebellious act was an attempt to find my voice and place in the world.

Growing up, I often felt caught between my family's expectations and my desire to break free and create my own path. My spirit of rebellion wasn't about rejecting my family or turning away from the values I'd been taught. Instead, it was my way of testing the boundaries around me. I wanted to know what life was like beyond the home I'd always known, and sometimes, that meant making decisions that others didn't agree with. Whether it led to a mistake or a small victory, each choice taught me something new about myself.

In those moments of defiance, I wasn't just rebelling against rules. I was searching for a deeper understanding of who I was becoming. Through these experiences, I started to learn about resilience, courage, and the power of making my own choices. My rebellious spirit became a journey of self-discovery that would eventually help me see the kind of person I wanted to be and the life I wanted to build.

Even today, I can see how those growing pains shaped me. They were necessary and helped me find my strength, even if I couldn't recognize it then. Rebellion taught me that understanding myself was a process that required both mistakes and moments of clarity. Through it all, I learned that true independence comes from knowing who you are and embracing the journey, no matter how difficult it might be.

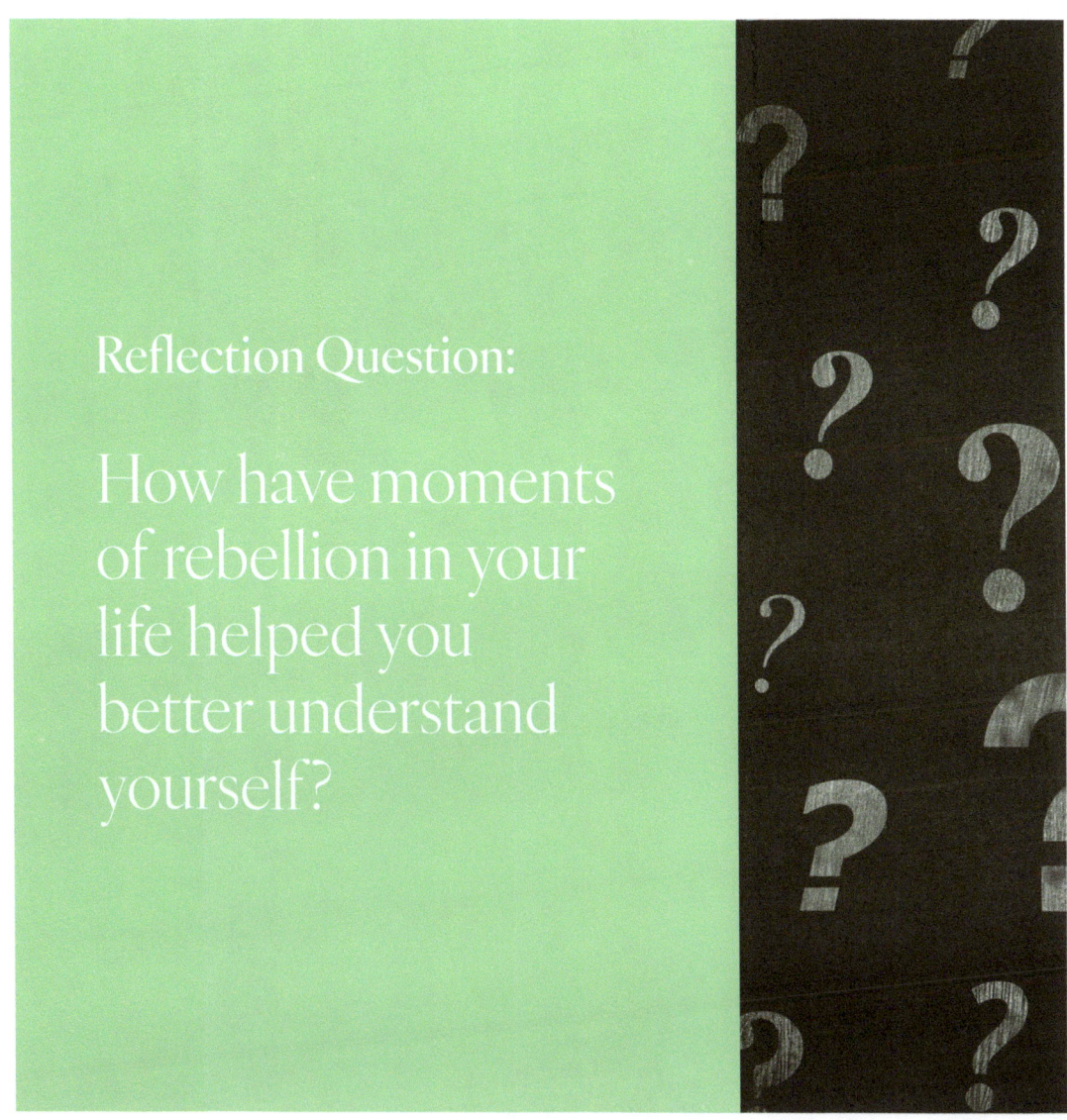

Reflection Question:

How have moments of rebellion in your life helped you better understand yourself?

Chapter 2:

The Joy of School Days

School was more than a place of academics for me. It was a haven, a world where I could escape and be myself. Those days were filled with laughter, friendship, and small moments of pride that I hold close to my heart. For me, school represented so much more than a place to learn from textbooks. It was where I formed some of my happiest memories, a place where I could experience joy, freedom, and a sense of belonging.

I became friends with Cassandra and Stephanie, my partners in every adventure. With them, I discovered the beauty of true friendship. Together, we shared secrets, dreams, and plans for the future. These friendships were more than just casual connections—they were bonds that helped me feel seen and understood. Through them, I learned how to trust and open my heart to others.

School also gave me moments of pride and achievement. Participating in events like the Spelling Bee, earning good grades, and receiving praise from teachers and classmates made me believe in myself. Each small success, every bit of recognition, boosted my confidence and helped me see that I had potential. School became a place where I was encouraged to dream, and those dreams gave me a sense of purpose.

As I reflect on those days, I realize how much those memories have shaped who I am. School was my safe place in a sometimes turbulent world, where I could experience pride in my accomplishments and connect with my classmates. Those joyful days taught me that even in difficult times, there are memories that bring light and happiness. The friendships and achievements I found there were gifts that continue to inspire me, reminding me of the power of small moments to shape our lives.

Rebellion, Reflection, and Renewal

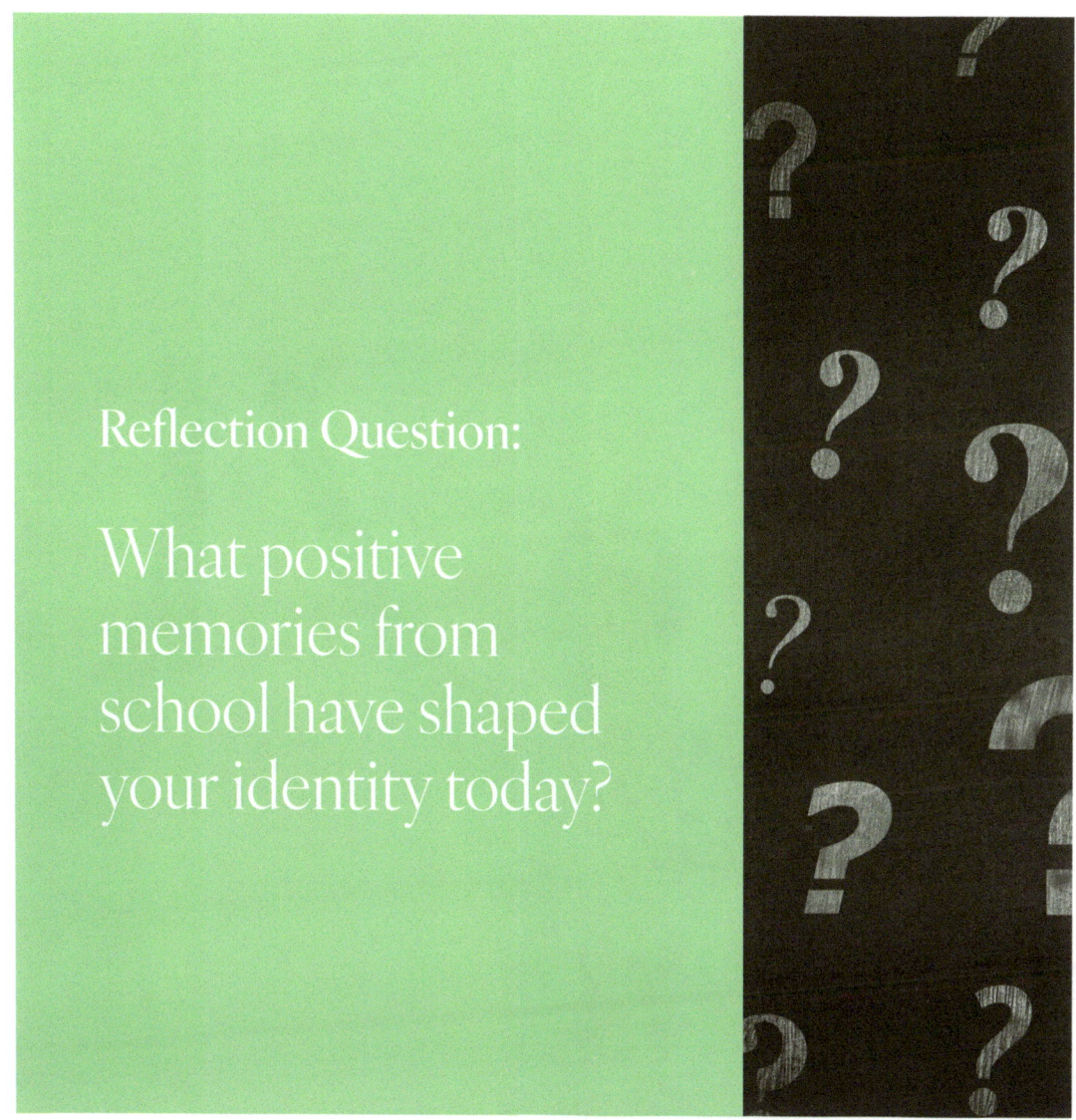

Reflection Question:

What positive memories from school have shaped your identity today?

Chapter 3:

Discovering Freedom Through Friendship

Friendship has a way of opening doors to parts of ourselves we might not know otherwise. Some of my friendships led me down paths I might not have chosen alone, but each one taught me something valuable. Through my friends, I learned about independence, loyalty, and the power of choice. These relationships allowed me to explore, make mistakes, and learn from them in ways I couldn't have imagined.

Some friends introduced me to experiences that weren't always wise, yet those moments were crucial to my growth. In these friendships, I learned what loyalty meant—not just loyalty to others but to myself and my values, too. Some friends helped me see what was truly important, even if I took a few stumbles along the way. They offered me a mirror, reflecting the kind of person I wanted to be and the values I wanted to uphold.

Through the freedom these friendships offered, I discovered the importance of making my own decisions. While not every choice led to the best outcomes, each one definitely shaped me. I learned that true independence isn't just about doing whatever you want—it's about choosing what's right for you, even if others don't agree. Friendships became a safe space for me to experiment, to understand my limits, and to explore who I was becoming.

Today, I can see how these relationships helped shape my decisions and guided my path. Each friendship, whether positive or challenging, taught me to navigate the world with a clearer sense of who I am. The freedom I discovered through friendship wasn't about following the crowd. It was about learning who I was and what mattered to me. Those early friendships were crucial and taught me that every choice has consequences and that absolute independence comes from honoring who I am.

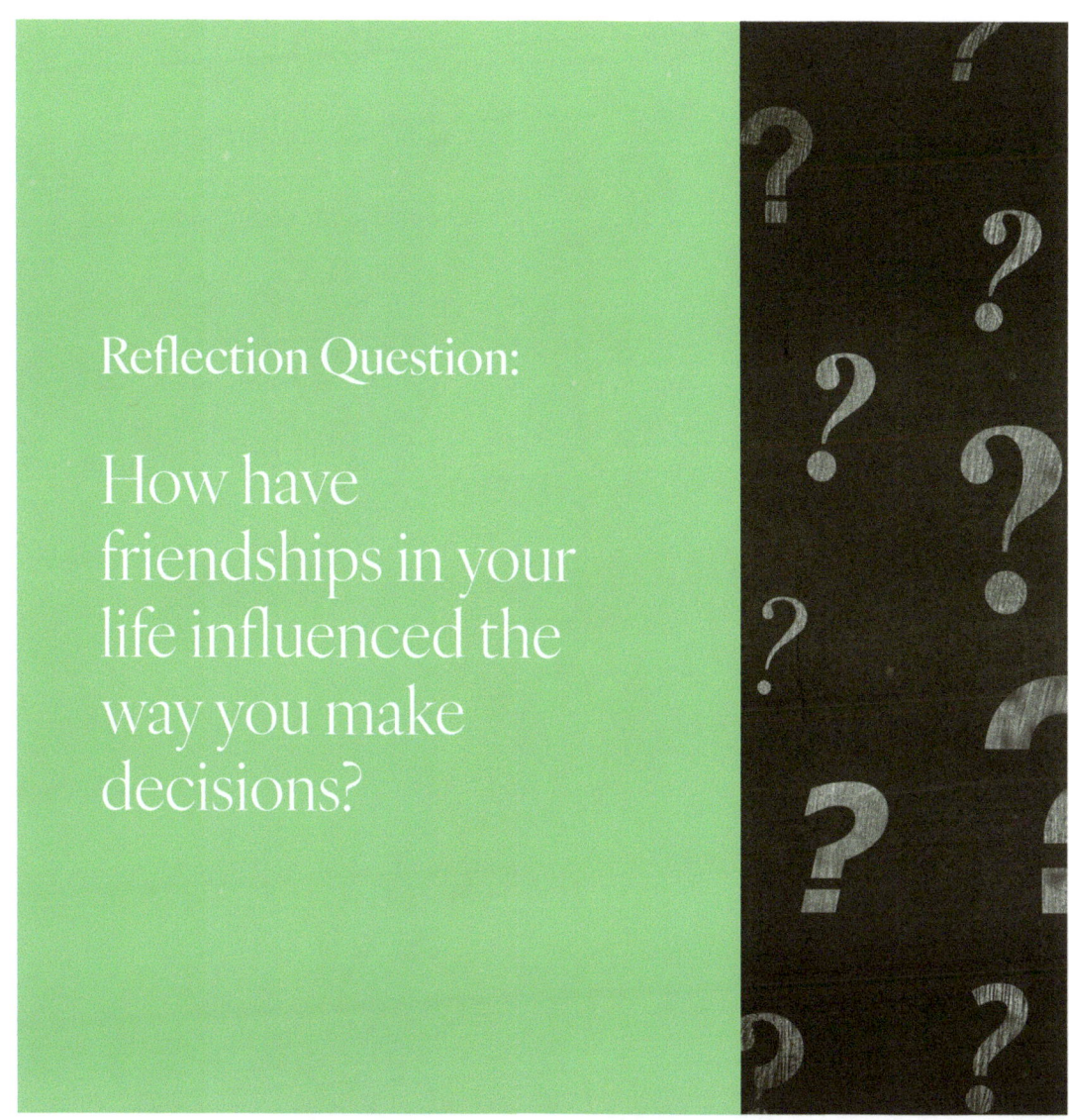

Reflection Question:

How have friendships in your life influenced the way you make decisions?

Chapter 4:

Lessons in Self-Discovery

Mistakes are often seen as failures, but I've come to understand them as stepping stones to growth. In my teenage years, I made choices that I would later regret—skipping school, drinking, lying, and smoking pot, to name a few. Yet, each misstep taught me something about myself, helping me see the person I wanted to become. Those mistakes weren't failures—they were moments of self-discovery, shaping my path in ways I couldn't foresee.

Growing up, I sometimes felt lost, unsure of who I was or what I wanted. Trying new things, even if they weren't the best choices, gave me insight into my identity. Each mistake, each rebellious act, revealed something new about my character. Through these experiences, I began to understand my values, limits, and dreams. I realized that mistakes are not something to be ashamed of but something to learn from.

I now see that each mistake pushed me to examine my actions and motivations. The rebellious choices I made forced me to question what truly mattered to me, even if I didn't understand it at the time. I learned that self-discovery is a journey that requires courage and compassion. I had to face my flaws, accept my missteps, and find a way to grow through them.

My rebellious phase became an exploration, a search for who I was beneath the layers of expectation and conformity. Whether right or wrong, each decision helped me peel back those layers and get closer to my authentic self. I began to understand that self-discovery wasn't about being perfect but about being honest with myself and learning from each experience.

Now, I look back on those years with gratitude. My mistakes weren't just bumps along the road—they were essential parts of my journey. They taught me that failure is not final and that each misstep is a chance to get closer to who we truly are. Every wrong turn helped me find my way, shaping the person I have become and reminding me that growth often comes through challenge and reflection.

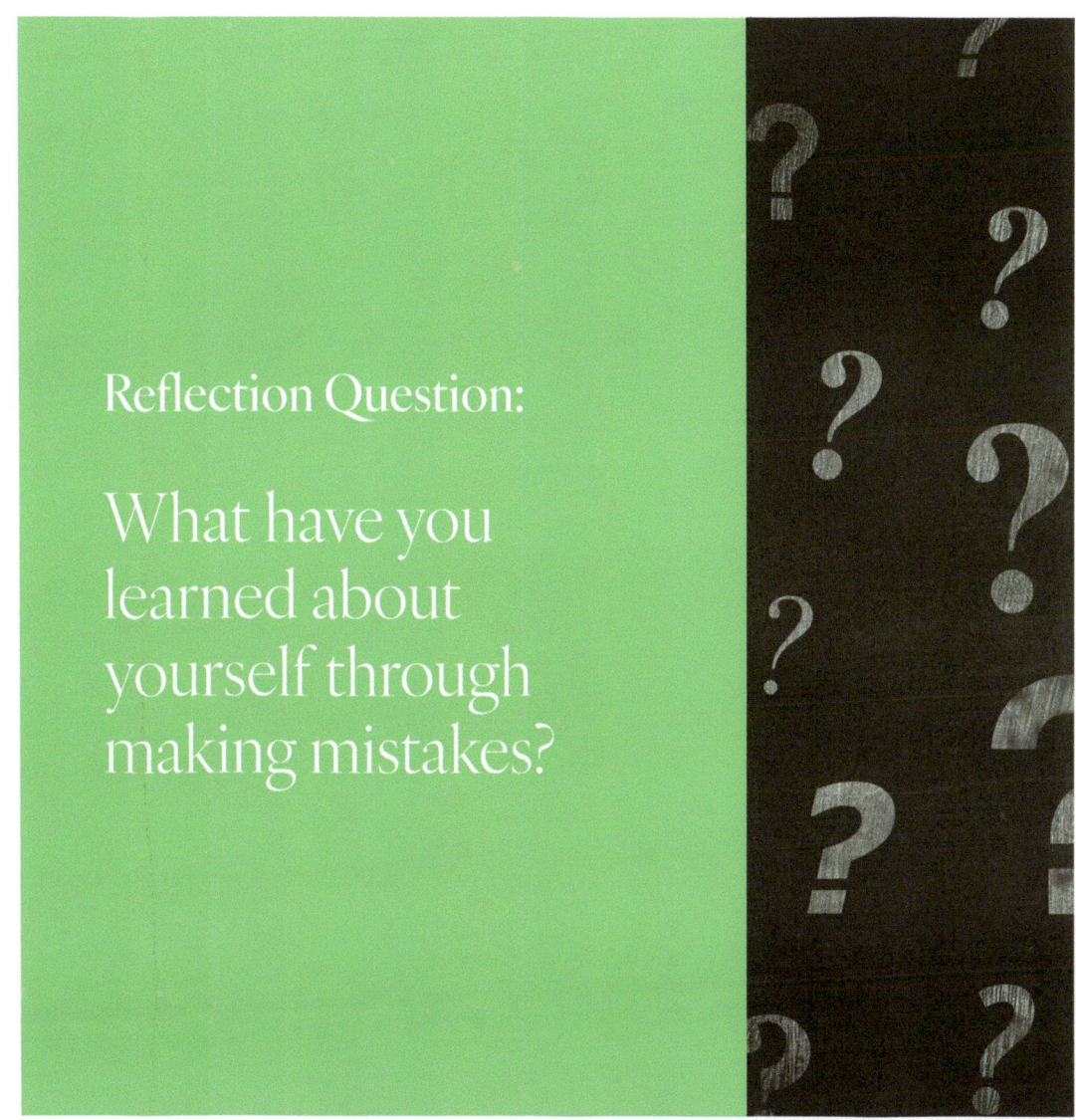

Reflection Question:

What have you learned about yourself through making mistakes?

Chapter 5:

Running Toward Independence

After dropping out of high school near the end of my junior year, running away from home when I was 16 was a bold, impulsive decision, but for me, it was a desperate bid for freedom. I wanted control over my life, a chance to make my own choices and to finally feel truly independent. I didn't know what lay ahead, but I knew I needed to break free. That moment of rebellion taught me valuable lessons about self-reliance, responsibility, and the reality of independence.

Leaving home wasn't as easy as I'd imagined. Living on my own, even temporarily, came with challenges I hadn't anticipated. Suddenly, I was responsible for things I'd always taken for granted—where I would sleep, what I would eat, and how I would take care of myself. Freedom, I discovered, wasn't just about escaping rules. It required a level of discipline and maturity I hadn't fully understood before. Each day brought new lessons, pushing me to grow up quickly.

During this time, I found myself relying on my instincts and resourcefulness. I had to learn to navigate situations I'd never faced, from finding safe places to stay to earning enough money to support myself. Though the experience was difficult, it also made me resilient. Each small victory—each day I managed on my own—helped me see that I was stronger than I thought.

My time away was a journey of self-discovery. I learned that independence wasn't just about escaping rules or avoiding authority. It was about understanding myself and taking responsibility for my actions. In facing the consequences of my decisions, I grew in ways I couldn't have imagined. I came to understand that true freedom is about building a life that reflects who you are and what you value.

I came to realize that running away was a turning point. It taught me that independence is both a gift and a responsibility, one that requires strength, resilience, and a willingness to face life's challenges head-on.

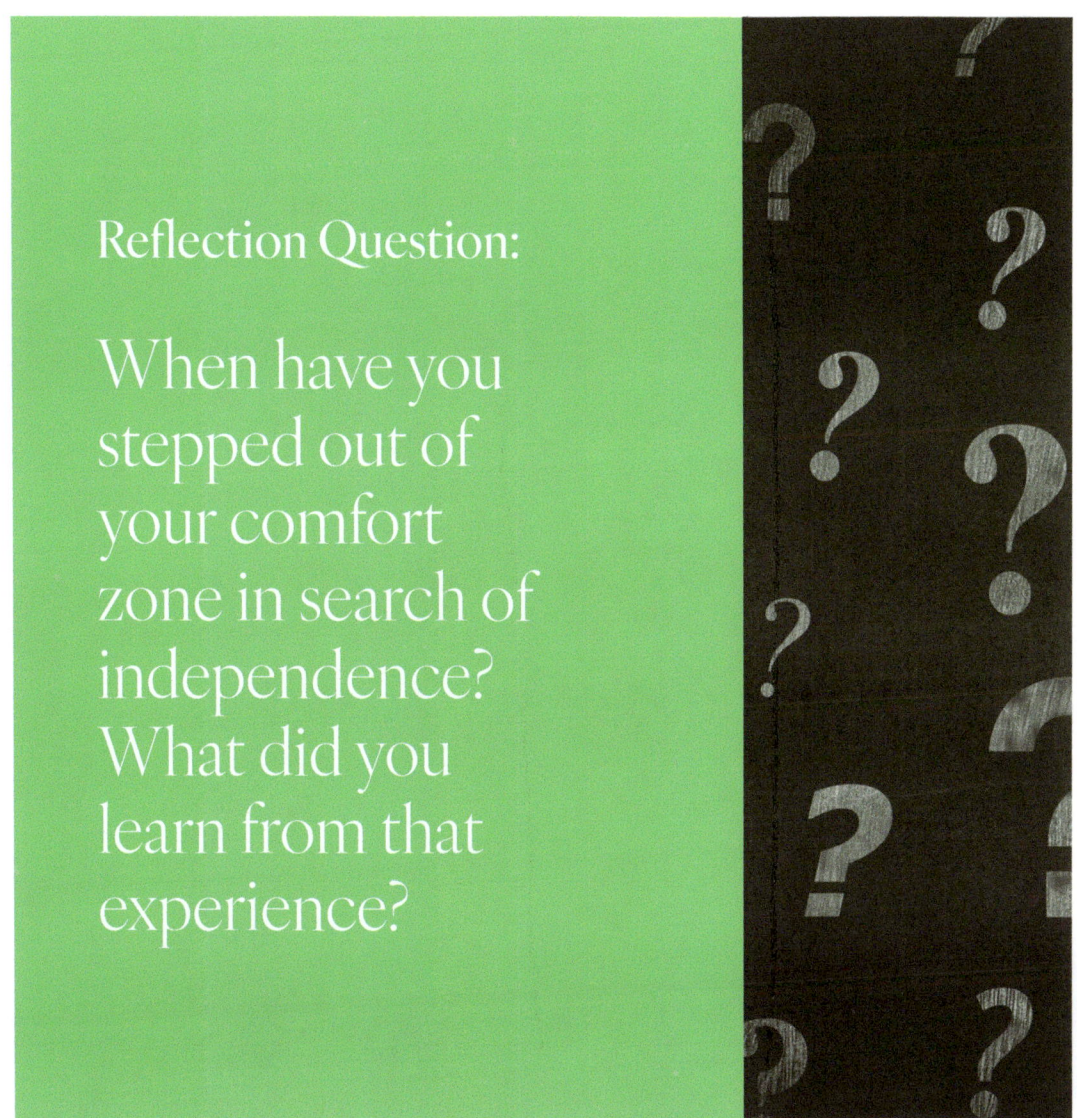

Reflection Question:

When have you stepped out of your comfort zone in search of independence? What did you learn from that experience?

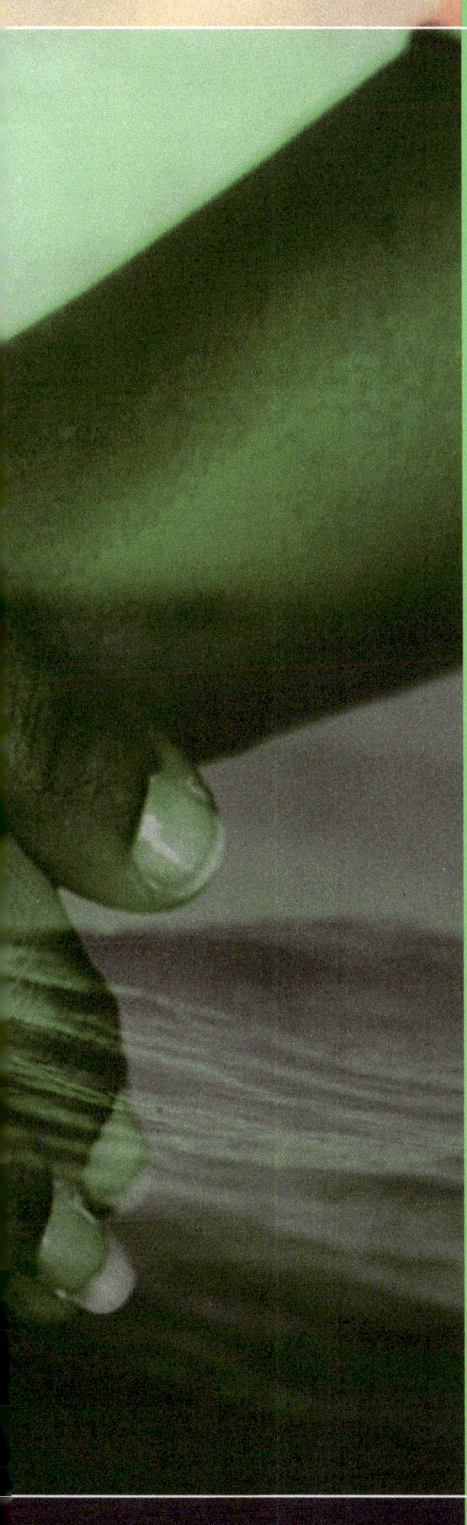

Chapter 6:

Finding Strength in Unexpected Places

When I left home, I wasn't sure where I'd go or who would help me, but I found support from an unexpected source. Tammy, a kind woman who opened her door to me, showed me that kindness often comes from people we least expect. Living with her taught me that sometimes strangers can offer the guidance and compassion we desperately need. Tammy's generosity was a lifeline, and her trust in me helped me believe in myself.

Tammy didn't just give me a place to stay; she offered me stability and warmth during a chaotic time. She didn't judge me for my past or question my decisions. Instead, she treated me with respect and kindness, teaching me that there is goodness in the world, even when we feel lost. Her support reminded me that we're never truly alone, and sometimes, help arrives from the most unlikely sources.

Through Tammy, I learned the importance of accepting help. I realized there's strength in leaning on others and allowing people to be there for us when we need it most. Her kindness gave me the courage to keep going, to see that I could still build a life for myself, no matter how broken I felt.

As I consider all that happened during that period in my life, I'm grateful for Tammy and for the lesson she taught me. She showed me that support doesn't always come from family or close friends—sometimes, it comes from the kindness of strangers. Her compassion changed my perspective, teaching me that we're all connected and that accepting help can be a powerful step toward healing.

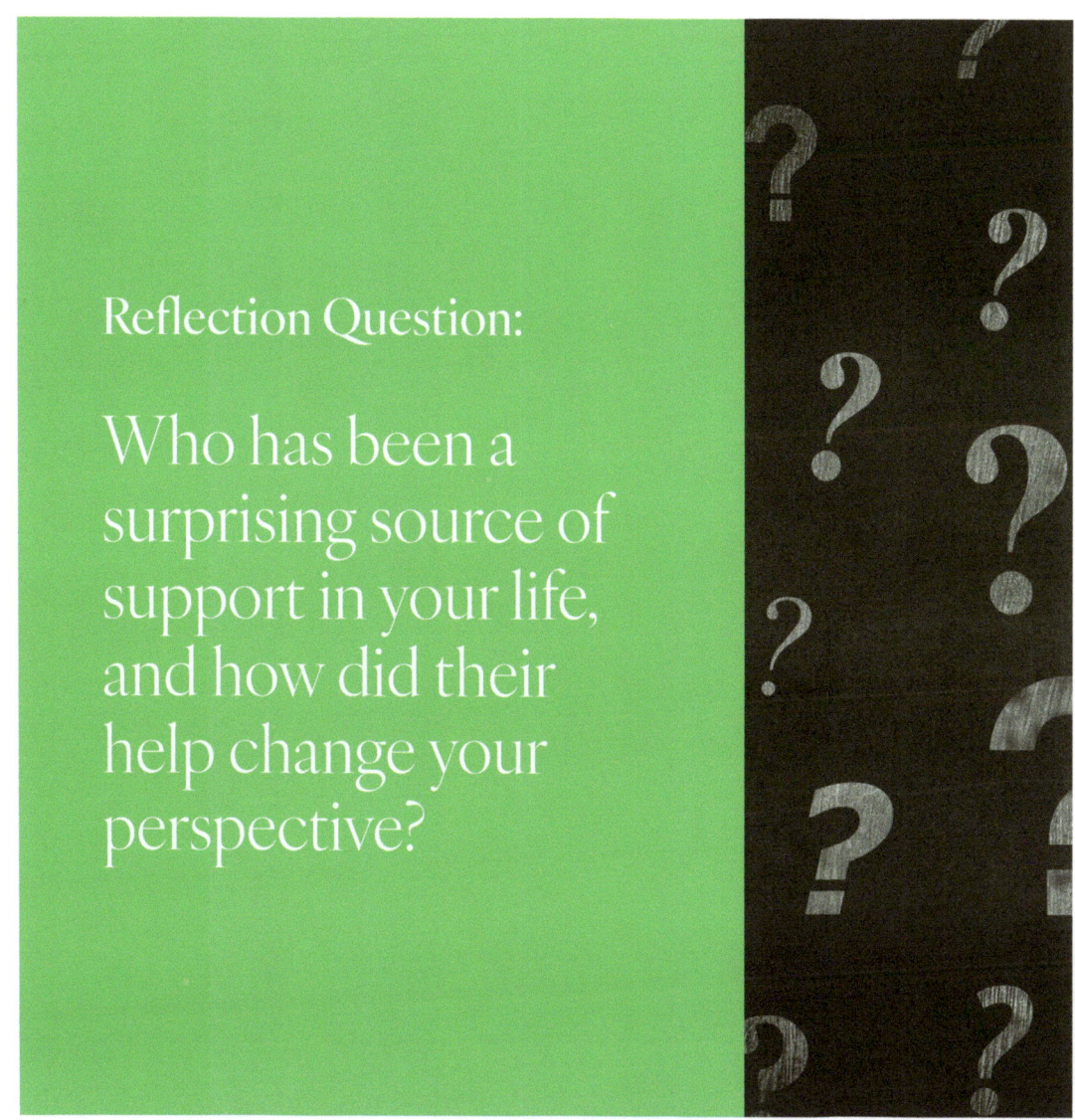

Reflection Question:

Who has been a surprising source of support in your life, and how did their help change your perspective?

Chapter 7:

The Redemption of Second Chances

Returning home wasn't the end of my journey. In many ways, it was just the beginning. After everything I'd been through, I realized that life often gives us second chances, but it's up to us to embrace them. Returning home was an opportunity to reset, learn from my past, and make better choices. It wasn't easy, but it helped me understand the value of forgiveness—both forgiving myself and others.

At first, I struggled with feelings of guilt and shame over the choices I had made and the pain I had caused my family. I wondered if I deserved a second chance or if I was capable of change. But over time, I began to see that forgiveness isn't about erasing mistakes—it's about accepting them, learning from them, and moving forward with a renewed sense of purpose. I started to forgive myself—not to let myself off the hook, but to release the heavy burden of regret holding me back.

Forgiving others was equally important. I held onto resentment and anger, believing those feelings protected me. However, I realized they only created walls, keeping me isolated from the people I needed most. Releasing that anger and choosing to forgive allowed me to reconnect with my family and those who had always cared for me.

Second chances taught me that redemption isn't about perfection but resilience and growth. Each new day offered an opportunity to start fresh and make decisions that aligned with the person I wanted to become. By taking responsibility for my actions and choosing a path of healing, I began to feel a sense of hope that I hadn't felt before.

I am grateful for the gift of second chances. They allowed me to rebuild my life, to move forward with compassion, and to see that we all have the power to change. Redemption isn't about forgetting the past—it's about transforming it into something meaningful and choosing to live with intention and purpose.

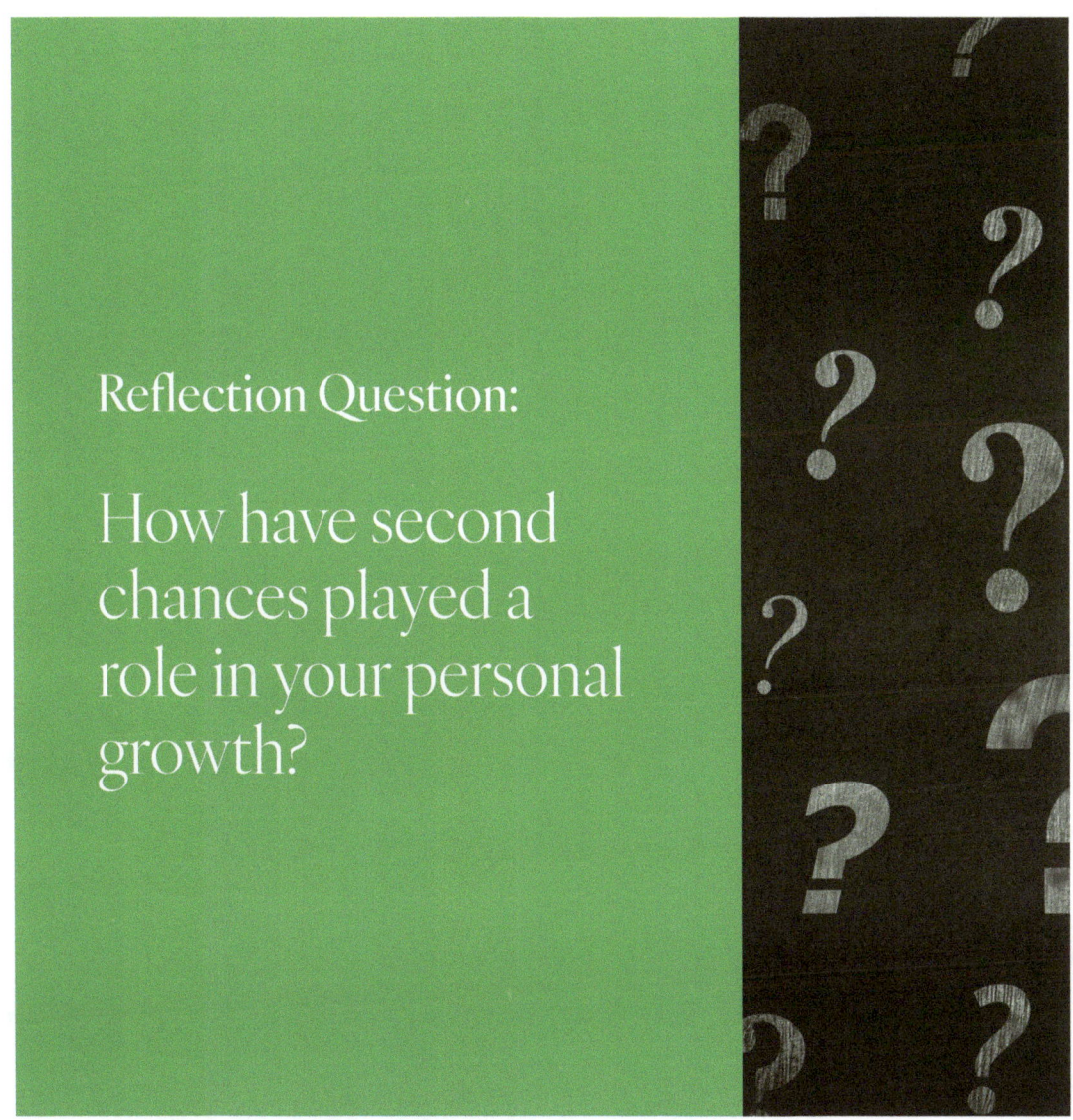

Reflection Question:

How have second chances played a role in your personal growth?

Chapter 8:

―

Embracing Change and Growth

Returning to school after all I had been through was a daunting experience, but it was also a powerful step toward reclaiming my life. I had to confront my fears and embrace the changes that came with stepping back into a structured environment. I knew that if I wanted to grow, I couldn't run from change—I had to welcome it and let it guide me forward. Going back to school became an opportunity to learn, not just academically but personally.

At first, I felt out of place. I wasn't the same person I had been before, and I worried about how others would see me. I carried the weight of my past, uncertain if I'd be accepted or judged. But over time, I realized that change wasn't something to fear—it was a pathway to becoming a better version of myself. Embracing this new chapter helped me gain confidence and resilience. With each class I attended, I saw that I could still achieve something meaningful, no matter where I had been before.

One of the most important lessons I learned was about resilience. I remembered how proud I'd felt in earlier years, like when I had worked hard for the Spelling Bee competition and felt the joy of success. Back then, the triumph came from my dedication and hard work, and I knew I could apply the same determination now. This memory became a source of strength for me as I navigated the challenges of returning to school. I realized that resilience is not about erasing the past but building on it and carrying forward the best parts of ourselves.

As I continued my journey, I grew stronger, more self-assured, and determined to build a future I could be proud of. Each day became a step toward becoming the person I knew I could be. Embracing change taught me to face life with courage, to welcome the unknown, and to trust in my ability to adapt.

I'm grateful for the chance to start again. Change taught me that growth is always possible and that even the most difficult moments can lead to transformation.

Reflection Question:

How has embracing change helped you grow as a person?

Chapter 9:

Rewriting My Story

Changing schools and working toward my GED was more than just an academic decision—it was a choice to rewrite my story. My past was filled with mistakes and missteps, but I didn't want those moments to define me. I wanted to prove that I could build a new path that reflected my goals and values. Earning my GED became a chance to take control of my narrative and show myself that I could create a better future.

Each day brought challenges, but with each class I completed, I felt a renewed sense of purpose. I wanted this change to be real, a new beginning that could carry me forward. I'd made choices that had led me down difficult paths, but I was determined to show myself that I had the strength to turn things around. Rewriting my story wasn't about erasing my past; it was about transforming those experiences into something positive.

As I worked through my classes, I often remembered the happy memories I had with my father when he called me "Pooh," my childhood nickname. I could still hear him cheering me on, and those memories became a source of motivation. I knew he would have wanted me to push forward and finish what I had started. His memory reminded me that I was capable of more and worthy of a better life. This small detail—a nickname from my childhood—symbolized the encouragement and support I still felt from those who loved me, even if they were no longer here.

Working toward my GED was about more than education. It was about reclaiming my power. I learned that we all have the ability to shape our lives and rewrite our stories, even after making mistakes. With each step I took toward my GED, I felt empowered, as if I was reclaiming parts of myself that I had lost along the way.

I am proud of the journey I took to rewrite my story. It was a reminder that no matter where we come from or what we've been through, we can always choose a different path. My journey to earn my GED showed me that redemption isn't about perfection—it's about resilience, growth, and the courage to start over.

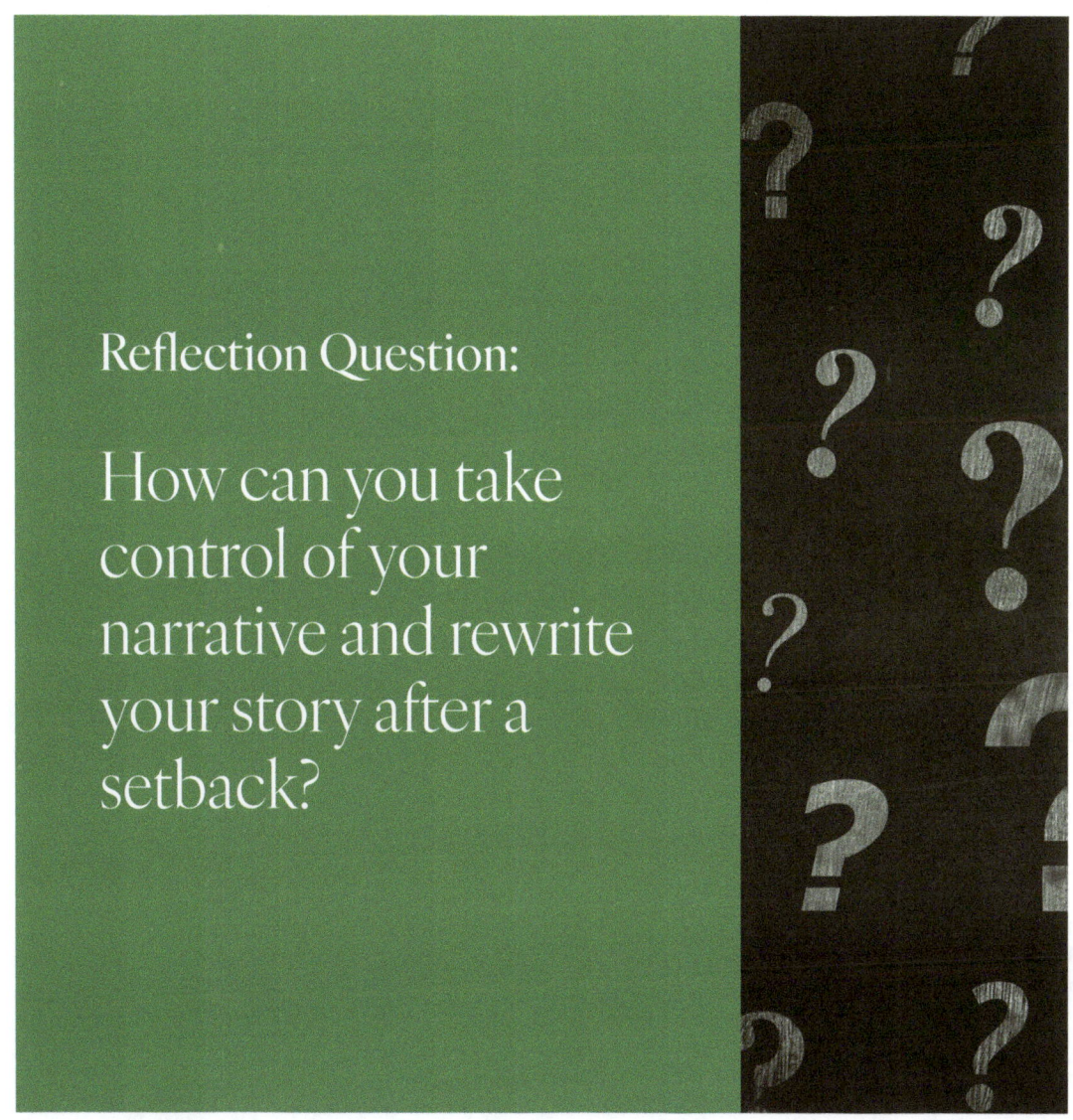

Reflection Question:

How can you take control of your narrative and rewrite your story after a setback?

Chapter 10:

Building Bridges, Not Walls

For a long time, I felt disconnected from my family. Our relationships were strained by misunderstandings, hurt, and unresolved conflicts. Each of us had been affected by the challenges we faced, and over time, we all built walls to protect ourselves from further pain. But as I grew older, I realized that holding onto resentment only isolates me from the people I needed most. I wanted to find a way to bridge those gaps, heal old wounds, and reconnect with my family in a meaningful way.

Rebuilding these relationships wasn't easy. It required patience, vulnerability, and a willingness to face the past honestly. One of the hardest parts was letting go of old grudges, especially the resentment I had carried toward my mother. I had blamed her for many things, including my father's absence, and that anger had become a barrier between us. But I knew I had to replace judgment with empathy if I wanted to move forward. I had to open myself up to forgiveness.

As I worked to mend my relationship with my family, I remembered the simple joys we once shared—like the times we spent with our neighbor Vanessa, whose kindness and care made us feel special and connected. Remembering those moments reminded me of the support we once shared, of the love that had been there even when life was complicated.

Slowly, the walls between us began to crumble, replaced by understanding and compassion. I saw that family bonds, though sometimes fragile, can be rebuilt with effort and honesty. By choosing to forgive and communicate openly, I found a path back to those I loved. My family and I had changed, but we could still find common ground and reconnect.

I'm grateful for the chance to build bridges with my family. Those relationships are now rooted in trust and acceptance, reminding me that healing is possible when we let go of anger and embrace forgiveness.

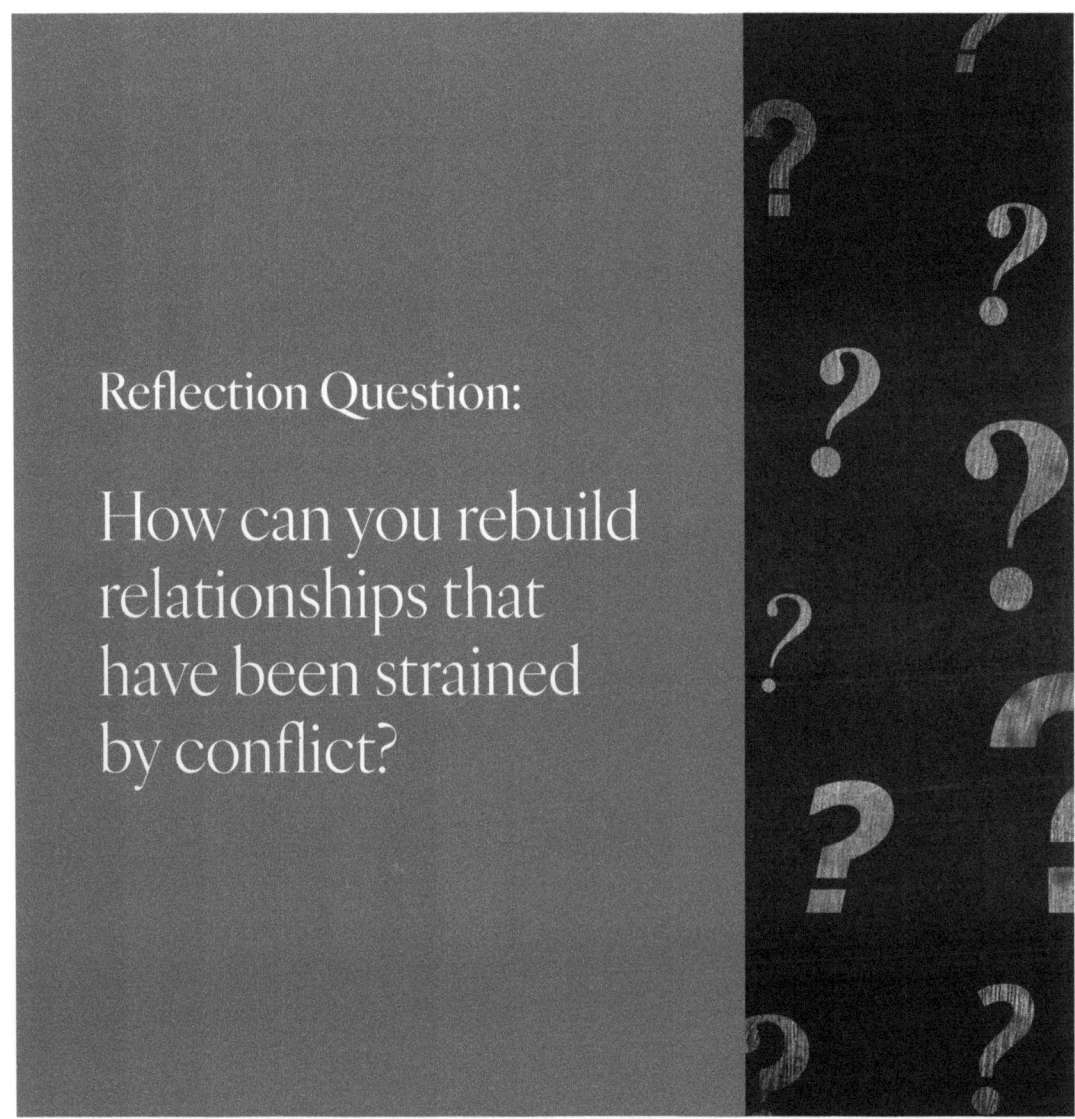

Reflection Question:

How can you rebuild relationships that have been strained by conflict?

Chapter 11:

Rediscovering My Strength

Earning my GED and exploring my interests in cosmetology and cooking were more than just accomplishments—they were stepping stones that helped me rediscover the strength I had within me all along. Through these experiences, I began to see that I could build a future that reflected my skills, interests, and dreams. Each new skill I learned, and each goal I reached reminded me that I could rely on myself to make things happen.

Cosmetology school was my first big step after earning my GED. I was fascinated by the art of transformation, of taking a simple canvas and creating something beautiful. Learning to style hair and give people confidence through their appearance gave me a sense of purpose. I loved practicing and experimenting with different techniques, seeing how I could bring my creativity to life. Although I eventually left cosmetology school, the skills I learned and the confidence I gained stayed with me. Cosmetology taught me that I could set my mind to something and make it real, an ability that would carry me through future challenges.

After cosmetology, I pursued another passion: cooking. I have always enjoyed the process of creating meals, and culinary school gave me a new appreciation for the art and precision that goes into every dish. I loved learning about flavors, techniques, and presentation. In the kitchen, I found a peaceful place to express myself. Cooking allowed me to connect with others and create something that brought people together. Completing my culinary certification was a moment of pride, proof that I could accomplish something meaningful.

These achievements were reminders of my strength and resilience. Cosmetology and cooking became symbols of my ability to rebuild my life, showing me that I could shape my future with my own hands. They reminded me that I was capable of more than I had ever believed.

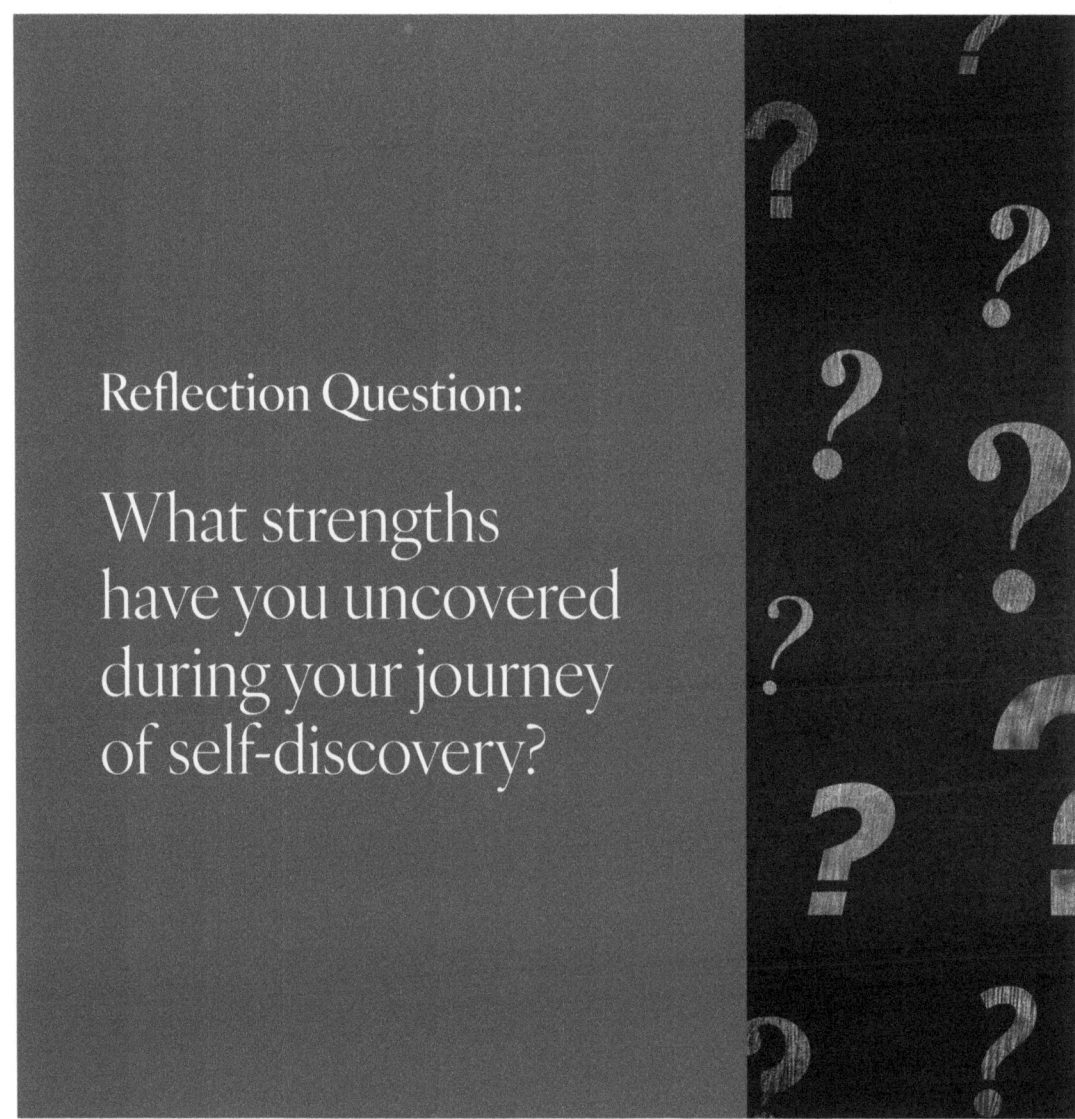

Reflection Question:

What strengths have you uncovered during your journey of self-discovery?

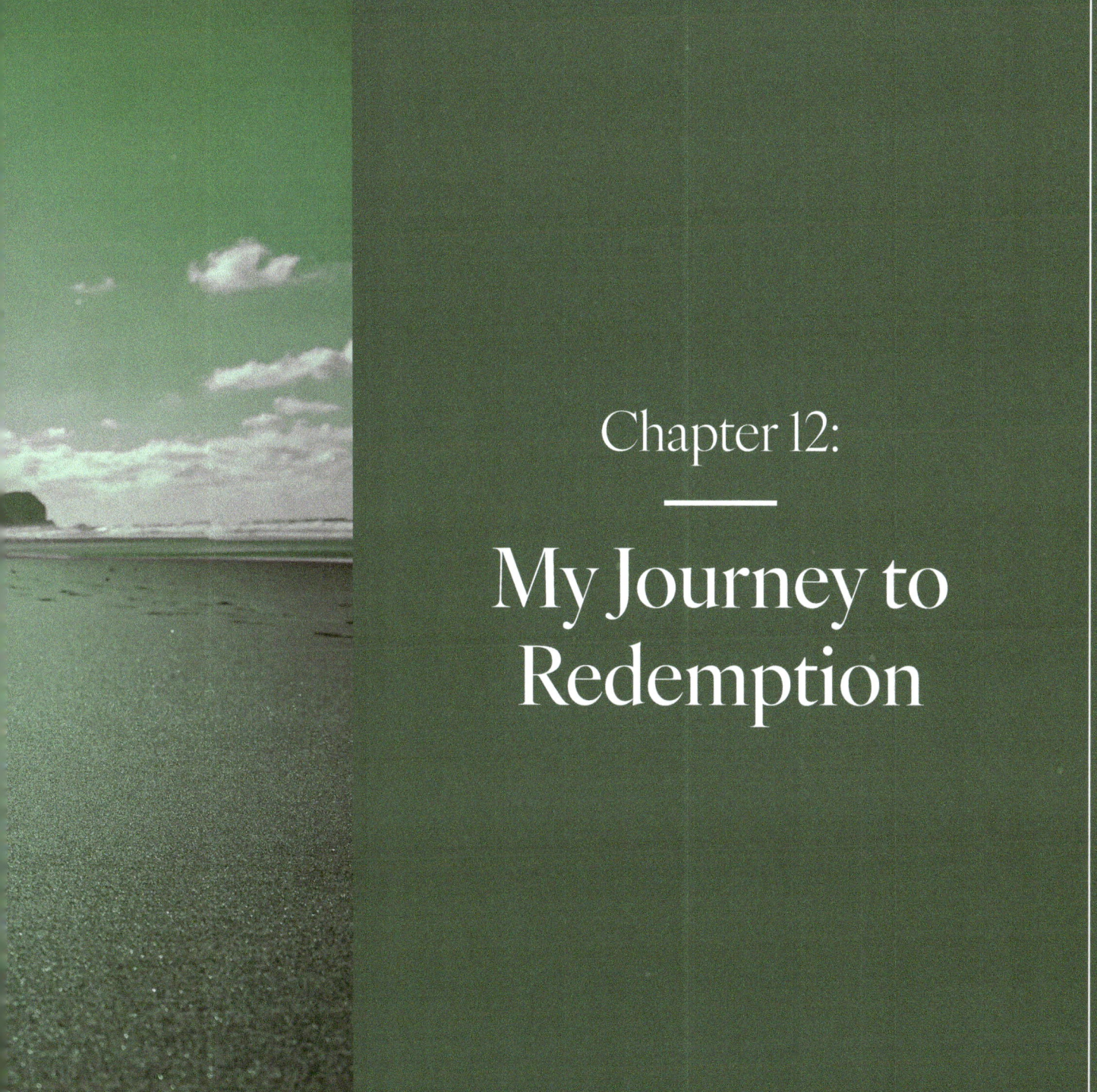

Chapter 12:

My Journey to Redemption

Redemption, for me, was about finding peace with my past and embracing hope for the future. My journey was filled with mistakes, regrets, and painful lessons, but over time, I learned that every experience, even the difficult ones, brought me closer to understanding my true self. I discovered that redemption isn't about erasing the past—it's about transforming it, using each lesson to guide me toward something better.

At first, seeing my past as anything other than a series of mistakes wasn't easy. But as I began to reflect, I saw the growth within each hardship. I learned that forgiving myself was a crucial part of healing. Each time I let go of regret, I made room for compassion and self-acceptance. With every choice I made to move forward, I felt myself letting go of old burdens, realizing they no longer had power over me.

This journey of redemption required me to embrace my mistakes and strengths. I learned that we're all capable of change, of building a life rooted in hope and purpose. It's a journey that begins by acknowledging where we've been and then choosing to focus on where we want to go. By finding peace with my past, I could step confidently into a future I could be proud of. This transformation wasn't sudden—it was a gradual process of learning to love myself as I was, flaws and all.

Looking back, I see that every challenge taught me resilience, every setback offered an opportunity for growth, and every choice led me closer to the person I am today. Redemption isn't a final destination—it's a continual commitment to live with intention and purpose, no matter where we start.

I've learned that we all have the power to rewrite our story. No matter what our past holds, we can take a step toward transformation. We have the ability to live a life that reflects our values, dreams, and true potential. All it takes is the courage to start.

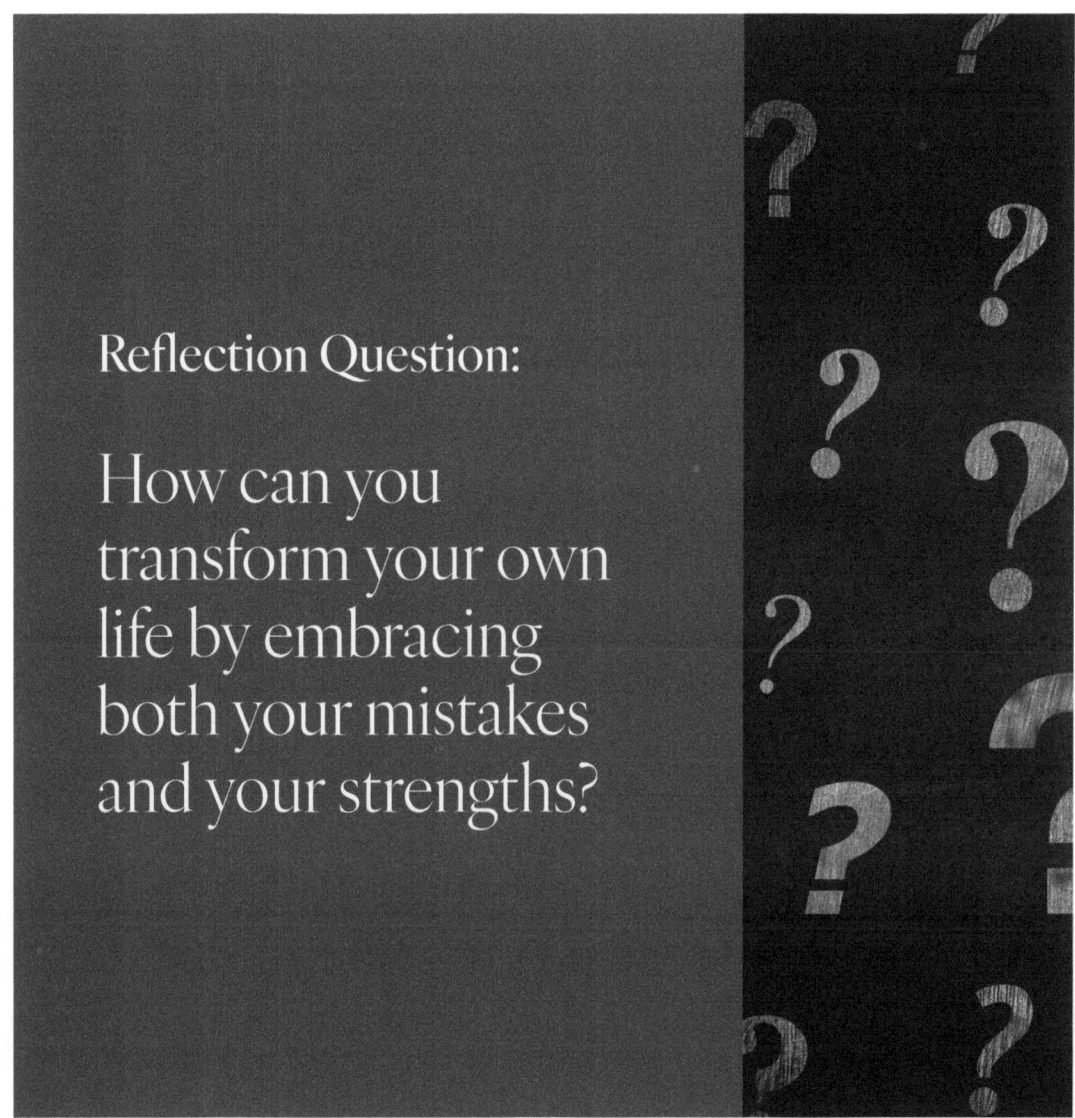

Reflection Question:

How can you transform your own life by embracing both your mistakes and your strengths?

About the Author

Sheresse Winford is a determined woman who is living her newfound life helping and inspiring others in every way she can. She loves to travel, and she takes a solo trip every year to renew her spiritual strength.

Volunteering and being of service to the community is a very important part of Sheresse's life. She makes time for that when she isn't working at her full-time job in finance as a senior collection specialist and small business owner of Intouch Painting and Debris Removal.

Most importantly, Sheresse says, *"I love God with all my heart and soul."*

www.ingramcontent.com/pod-product-compliance
Lightning Source LLC
Chambersburg PA
CBHW062022050526
44107CB00106B/955